HQ

D0857614

WATERFOWL

WATERFOWL

DAVE BEATY
THE CHILD'S WORLD

CONTENTS

The waterfowl family consists of ducks, geese, and swans. These aquatic, web-footed birds come in all sizes, shapes, and colors. They live throughout the world.

Ducks are the smallest waterfowl. They range in size from foot-long buffleheads to mallards and mergansers, which grow to be over two feet long. Male ducks are called *drakes*. They have more colorful feathers than the dull plumage of the females, or *hens*. Like other waterfowl, ducks are mainly vegetarians, though some species eat crustaceans, insects, and fish they find in the water.

Geese are larger than ducks, and

have much longer necks. Unlike ducks, male and female geese look alike, and the males are called *ganders*, not drakes. As with other waterfowl, geese gather in large flocks each autumn. They travel long distances to spend the winter in warm climates.

Swans are the largest members of the waterfowl family. They have very long necks and large bodies, and most have snow-white feathers. While people throughout the world hunt ducks and geese, swans are protected by law in most countries.

The following are some of the water-fowl species that live in North America.

7

MALLARD DUCKS

Mallard ducks are probably the best-known species of waterfowl in North America. These colorful birds are often called greenheads because of the drakes' bright green head feathers. Mallards eat plants growing on the edges of lakes, ponds, and rivers. They also eat underwater vegetation by *dabbling*. Tipping themselves forward, the ducks plunge their heads completely underwater. Then, by stretching their necks, they pluck vegetation from the lake bottom. During fall migration, mallards sometimes stop in fields to eat seeds and grasses.

Wood Ducks

Unlike most waterfowl, wood ducks build their nests in trees, often using large woodpecker holes. After the eggs hatch, the young ducks struggle to climb out of the hole. With quacks of encouragement from the mother hen, the ducklings plunge to the ground below. As a reward, the hen takes her chicks to a nearby pond for their first swim. Plants growing near woodland ponds are the main food source for wood ducks, though they also eat seeds and nuts. Many consider the male wood duck one of the world's most beautiful birds.

PINTAIL DUCKS

Pintail ducks are named for their pointed tails and wingtips. These alert birds zip through the air like feathered jets. They share many characteristics with mallards, although pintails spend less time on the ground. Like mallards, pintails are surface-feeders, or *dabblers*. Pintails have the widest breeding range of any duck. They live all over the United States, though they are most common in the western states. Mother pintails are very protective of their young. They even attack people who wander too close to their nests!

CANVASBACK DUCKS

Canvasback ducks are the star athletes of the water-fowl family. They dive underwater for food and to escape danger. Before taking flight, the ducks run along the top of the water. Once airborne, canvas-backs rank among the fastest-flying ducks on the continent. Long, powerful wings carry them at speeds of up to seventy miles per hour. Canvasbacks spend summers in the lakes, ponds, and marshes of the northern woods. When autumn approaches, they seek saltwater marshes and bays along the coastlines of the United States and Mexico.

BUFFLEHEAD DUCKS

Buffleheads are one of the smallest ducks in North America. Because their heads are large compared to the rest of their bodies, they are sometimes called buffaloheads. Although buffleheads are diving ducks, they jump out of the water to fly, much like dabblers do. They build their nests in trees close to open water. Because they are small, buffleheads are vulnerable to predators. Eagles, hawks, and owls swoop down from above, while fish such as muskellunge, pike, and bass are a constant threat from below.

RUDDY DUCKS

Ruddy ducks are one of the few stiff-tailed ducks in North America. Their broad, fan-shaped tails and small bodies make them easy to identify in the wild. The female ruddy is about one-third the size of a mallard hen. Although their small wings help them fly very fast, ruddy ducks prefer to stay in the water. They are excellent divers. When in danger, ruddy ducks dive underwater and swim away to safety. These ducks prefer to eat weeds growing on lake bottoms. If weeds are scarce, they eat insects and crustaceans.

MERGANSERS

Mergansers have long, slender bodies that make diving and swimming nearly effortless. They also have sharp, backward-facing teeth that help them catch and hold fish—their favorite meal. Female mergansers sometimes lay their eggs in occupied wood-duck nests. Then both hens help watch over the eggs. There are three types of mergansers—the common, the red-breasted, and the hooded. The hooded merganser, shown in this photograph, is the smallest of the three species. The crest on its head is not found on any other species of waterfowl.

CANADA GEESE

The Canada goose is probably the best-known goose in North America. However, few people realize that there are twelve different types of Canada geese. The giant Canada goose shown in this photograph is the largest. Except for size, all Canada geese look and behave alike. In fact, they usually flock and migrate together in the fall. Canada geese are one of the few birds that make noise while flying. They make loud, honking sounds to communicate with each other in the air. For this reason, they are often called Canadian honkers.

Snow Geese

Snow geese are truly northern birds. They spend summers in the far northern reaches of Alaska, Canada, and Greenland. As winter sets in on these Arctic lands, snow geese begin their southward migration. The greater snow goose is larger than its relative, the lesser snow goose. Greater snow geese usually migrate down the east coast of North America. They spend winters along the Atlantic coast, as far south as North Carolina. Lesser snow geese prefer the Pacific coast, sometimes migrating as far south as the Baja Peninsula.

TRUMPETER SWANS

These beautiful birds are named for their unique, trumpetlike call. Of all North American waterfowl, trumpeter swans are the largest. Adults stand four feet tall and can weigh as much as two bowling balls! Watching these huge birds fly in formation is a remarkable sight. Because of their size, trumpeter swans were a prized game bird to the early settlers. As a result, the birds were nearly wiped out. Today hunting swans is illegal, and trumpeters are no longer endangered. Southeastern Alaska is their primary breeding ground.

MUTE SWANS

Mute swans are only slightly smaller than trumpeters. While trumpeter swans are native to the continent, mute swans were introduced in North America many years ago. The birds now live wild along the Atlantic coast. Mute swans have unusual bills. Orange with a black tip and a large black knob at its base, the bill is hard to mistake! When flying, the swans' large, powerful wings make a beautiful melody as they slice through the air. These swans often float on ponds and lakes with their necks in a definite S shape.

PHOTO RESEARCH

Charles Rotter / Archipelago Productions

PHOTO CREDITS

Joe McDonald: front cover, 9

Tom & Pat Leeson: 2, 6-7, 11, 15, 21, 23, 27

Jeanne Drake: 4, 13, 17, 25, 31

Robert & Linda Mitchell: 19

E. R. Degginger: 29

Library of Congress Cataloging-in-Publication Data
Beaty, Dave, 1965-
Waterfowl / by Dave Beaty.
p.   cm.
Summary: Describes the physical characteristics, habits,
and behavior of a variety of waterfowl species. Includes
ducks, geese, and swans.
ISBN 1-56766-006-1
1. Waterfowl--Juvenile literature.
2. Ducks--Juvenile literature.   3. Geese--Juvenile literature
4. Swans--Juvenile literature
[1. Water birds. 2. Ducks. 3. Geese. 4. Swans.]   I. Title.
QL696.A52B43   1993   92-32319
598.4'1--dc20   CIP
                                                      AC

Distributed to schools and libraries in the United States by
ENCYCLOPAEDIA BRITANNICA EDUCATIONAL CORP.
310 South Michigan Avenue
Chicago, Illinois 60604